BASEBALL LEGENDS

Hank Aaron
Grover Cleveland Alexander
Ernie Banks
Johnny Bench
Yogi Berra
Roy Campanella
Roberto Clemente
Ty Cobb
Dizzy Dean
Joe DiMaggio
Bob Feller
Jimmie Foxx
Lou Gehrig
Bob Gibson
Rogers Hornsby
Walter Johnson
Sandy Koufax
Mickey Mantle
Christy Mathewson
Willie Mays
Stan Musial
Satchel Paige
Brooks Robinson
Frank Robinson
Jackie Robinson
Babe Ruth
Duke Snider
Warren Spahn
Willie Stargell
Honus Wagner
Ted Williams
Carl Yastrzemski
Cy Young

CHELSEA HOUSE PUBLISHERS

BASEBALL LEGENDS

SANDY KOUFAX

John Grabowski

Introduction by
Jim Murray

Senior Consultant
Earl Weaver

CHELSEA HOUSE PUBLISHERS
New York • Philadelphia

Published by arrangement with
Chelsea House Publishers.
Newfield Publications is a federally
registered trademark of Newfield
Publications, Inc.

Produced by James Charlton Associates
New York, New York.

Designed by Hudson Studio
Ossining, New York.

Typesetting by LinoGraphics
New York, New York.

Picture research by Carolann Hawkins
Cover illustration by Dan O'Leary

Library of Congress Cataloging-in-Publication Data

Grabowski, John F.
    Sandy Koufax / John Grabowski; introduction by Jim Murray;
senior consultant Earl Weaver.
      p. cm.—(Baseball legends)
    Includes bibliographical references (p.   ) and index.
    Summary: A biography of Hall of Fame baseball player Sandy
Koufax, the greatest left-handed pitcher in Dodgers history.
    ISBN 0-7910-1180-1.—ISBN 0-7910-1214-X (pbk.)
    1. Koufax, Sandy, 1935- —Juvenile literature. 2. Baseball
players—United States—Biography—Juvenile literature. 3. Los
Angeles Dodgers (Baseball team)—Juvenile literature. [1. Koufax,
Sandy, 1935- . 2. Baseball players. 3. Los Angeles Dodgers
(Baseball team)] I. Title. II. Series.
GV865.K67G73 1991   91-519
796.357'092—dc20   CIP
  [B]   AC

CONTENTS

WHAT MAKES A STAR

Jim Murray

No one has ever been able to explain to me the mysterious alchemy that makes one man a .350 hitter and another player, more or less identical in physical makeup, hard put to hit .200. You look at an Al Kaline, who played with the Detroit Tigers from 1953 to 1974. He was pale, stringy, almost poetic-looking. He always seemed to be struggling against a bad case of mononucleosis. But with a bat in his hands, he was King Kong. During his career, he hit 399 home runs, rapped out 3,007 hits, and compiled a .297 batting average.

Form isn't the reason. The first time anybody saw Roberto Clemente step into the batter's box for the Pittsburgh Pirates, the best guess was that Clemente would be back in Double A ball in a week. He had one foot in the bucket and held his bat at an awkward angle—he looked as though he couldn't hit an outside pitch. A lot of other ballplayers may have had a better-looking stance. Yet they never led the National League in hitting in four different years, the way Clemente did.

Not every ballplayer is born with the ability to hit a curveball. Nor is exceptional hand-eye coordination the key to heavy hitting. Big-league locker rooms are filled with players who have all the attributes, save one: discipline. Every baseball man can tell you a story about a pitcher who throws a ball faster than anyone has ever seen but who has no control on or *off* the field.

The Hall of Fame is full of people who transformed themselves into great ballplayers by working at the sport, by studying the game, and making sacrifices. They're overachievers—and winners. If you want to find them, just watch the World Series. Or simply read about New York Yankee great Lou Gehrig; Ted Williams, "the Splendid Splinter" of the Boston Red Sox; or the Dodgers' strikeout king Sandy Koufax.

A pitcher *should* be able to win a lot of ballgames with a 98-miles-per-hour fastball. But what about the pitcher who wins 20 games a year with a fastball so slow that you can catch it with your teeth? Bob Feller of the Cleveland Indians got into the Hall of Fame with a blazing fastball that glowed in the dark. National League star Grover Cleveland Alexander got there with a pitch that took considerably longer to reach the plate; but when it did arrive, the pitch was exactly where Alexander wanted it to be—and the last place the batter expected it to be.

There are probably more players with exceptional ability who didn't make it to the major leagues than there are who did. A number of great hitters, bored with fielding practice, had to be dropped from their team because their home-run production didn't make up for their lapses in the field. And then there are players like Brooks Robinson of the Baltimore Orioles, who made himself into a human vacuum cleaner at third base because he knew that working hard to become an expert fielder would win him a job in the big leagues.

A star is not something that flashes through the sky. That's a comet. Or a meteor. A star is something you can steer ships by. It stays in place and gives off a steady glow; it is fixed, permanent. A star works at being a star.

And that's how you tell a star in baseball. He shows up night after night and takes pride in how brightly he shines. He's Willie Mays running so hard his hat keeps falling off; Ty Cobb sliding to stretch a single into a double; Lou Gehrig, after being fooled in his first two at-bats, belting the next pitch off the light tower because he's taken the time to study the pitcher. Stars never take themselves for granted. That's why they're stars.

1

THE TURNING POINT

The turning point in the career of a professional baseball player may occur at any time and any place.

In the case of a hard-throwing, 25-year-old left-handed pitcher named Sandy Koufax, that pivotal moment occurred during a plane flight to Orlando, Florida, in the spring of 1961. Koufax was traveling south with his Los Angeles Dodgers teammates for an exhibition game against the Minnesota Twins. The game was to feature the Dodgers' second-string players; the regulars would be playing the Detroit Tigers in nearby Lakeland that same day.

Koufax had been with the Dodgers since signing a bonus contract in 1954. Though arguably the hardest thrower in the big leagues, the lanky left-hander had not yet been able to harness his amazing talent. While he had averaged nearly one strikeout per inning in his career, he had also been plagued by wildness, averaging

Coach Joe Becker instructs the Dodgers pitchers during the 1957 spring training at Vero Beach, Florida. Koufax (third from right, wearing a jacket) listens intently.

more than five walks for every nine innings pitched. The end result was a record of 36 wins and 40 losses in his six years with the team. But now, at the start of his seventh season, all that was about to change.

Sitting next to Koufax on the flight to Orlando was his roommate, catcher Norm Sherry. The two players had often discussed Koufax's control problems. It was Sherry's belief that much of his roommate's trouble came from overthrowing—trying to work his way out of tough situations by attempting to overpower opposing batters. He had said this to Koufax more than once, and as the plane began its descent, he said it again.

"If you get behind the hitter, don't try to throw hard, because when you force your fastball, you're always high with it. Just this once, try it my way like we've talked about."

Koufax had heard it all many times before: Ease up. . .don't press . . .relax. . .don't over-throw. But this time, for some reason, he was ready to listen.

Minnesota was a hard-hitting team. The Twins had belted out 147 home runs the previous year (when the franchise was known as the Washing-ton Senators), ranking fourth in that category behind only the powerful New York Yankees, the Milwaukee Braves, and the Detroit Tigers. The club was led by future Hall of Famer Harmon Killebrew and Jim Lemon, who had combined to hit 69 homers between them. But there would be no home runs for any of the Twins in this game.

Following Sherry's directions, Koufax quickly got ahead of the batters, then made them go after the pitch he wanted them to hit. The results were dramatic. Koufax hurled seven hitless innings before being removed.

To celebrate his "discovery," Koufax and pitcher Larry Sherry—Norm's brother—went out to a movie when the team returned to Vero Beach, where the Dodgers' spring training camp was located. After the film, the two discussed the craft of pitching over pizza.

By the time they made their way back to camp, it was an hour past curfew. Their late arrival resulted in a fine of $100 apiece, but Koufax had no complaints. He already knew the value of the lesson he had learned the previous day. It was like having a light switch turned on after spending years in darkness.

The seasons 1961 through 1966 saw Koufax emerge as the dominant pitcher in the game. He won an incredible 73 percent of his decisions (129 wins and 47 losses), hurled 4 no-hitters (including a perfect game), and won an unprecedented 5 consecutive earned-run-average (ERA) titles. All told, upon his retirement his career record stood at 165–87; his career .655 winning percentage is the 10th best on the all-time list.

Were it not for the advice of a second-string catcher, Sandy Koufax might well have gone down in baseball annals as a pitcher whose actual performance fell far short of his potential. Instead, Sandy Koufax, when on top of his game, may have been the best pitcher of them all.

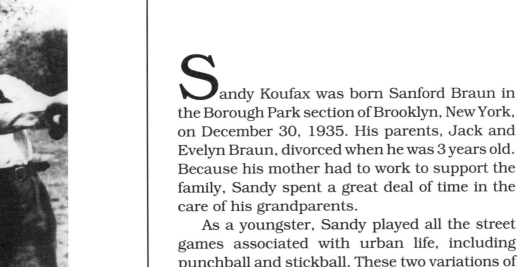

Sandy Koufax was born Sanford Braun in the Borough Park section of Brooklyn, New York, on December 30, 1935. His parents, Jack and Evelyn Braun, divorced when he was 3 years old. Because his mother had to work to support the family, Sandy spent a great deal of time in the care of his grandparents.

As a youngster, Sandy played all the street games associated with urban life, including punchball and stickball. These two variations of baseball involved hitting a rubber ball with a clenched fist or a broomstick—equipment readily available to city kids.

When Sandy was 9 years old, his mother married a prominent New York lawyer named Irving Koufax, and the family moved to Rockville Centre on Long Island. The suburban New York town was like the country to a Jewish boy from Brooklyn. With more room available, ball fields

Eight-year-old Sandy, hitting righthanded, demonstrates the swing that would give him an .097 career batting average in the major leagues.

replaced streets and schoolyards as the scenes of Sandy's sporting triumphs. He adapted well and was voted Athlete of the Year at the Morris School in 1943 and again in 1945.

In 1946, however, Sandy's athletic career almost came to an end. Soon after receiving a bicycle as a 10th-birthday present from his grandparents, he was involved in an accident. Swerving to avoid an automobile, he was hit on the knee. The injury caused him to miss one complete football season but, luckily, had no lasting effect.

On the day Sandy graduated from ninth grade, the Koufax family moved back to Brooklyn, settling in the Bensonhurst section of the borough. Basketball became his favorite sport, and by 1952, his senior year at Lafayette High School, he was named captain of the school team.

One time, several members of the New York Knickerbockers basketball team played a benefit game against Lafayette in the school's gymnasium. One of Sandy's heroes, Knicks center Harry Gallatin, was so impressed with the youngster's performance that he told Lafayette coach Frank Rabinowitz, "I wouldn't be surprised if we come back for that kid one of these days. He has a real future in pro basketball."

Meanwhile, Sandy was also developing his skills on the baseball diamond. Lafayette enjoyed a long and hallowed sports tradition, with Bob Giallombardo, Bob and Ken Aspromonte, Jerry Casale, Larry Ciaffone, Larry Yellen, and Al Ferrara numbering among alumni who had graduated to the major leagues, as well as current relief star John Franco.

The Lafayette team already had several good pitchers, including Fred Wilpon, who eventually

SANDY KOUFAX

UC pitcher, 1954
Bearcat Freshman basketball, 1953–54

Major league baseball Player of the
Decade, 1960–69

Cy Young Award winner three times,
1963–65–66

Pitched four no-hitters from 1962–65
(one perfect game.)

Holds major league single season
strikeout record of 382 (1965)

Best ERA in National League a record
five consecutive years, 1962–66

Averaged more than one strikeout per inning
pitched for career with Los Angeles (Brooklyn)
Dodgers, 1955–66

National League Most Valuable Player
1963

Last four seasons:
27–9, 26–8, 19–5, 25–5

Lifetime record: 165-87 · · 2.76 ERA

Pitching for the University of Cincinnati, Koufax once struck out 18 batters, a school record, against the University of Louisville.

went on to become president and chief executive officer of the New York Mets. Sandy tried out as a first baseman and made the squad.

Although Sandy's batting left much to be desired, he possessed a live throwing arm. It was this arm that caught the eye of Milt Laurie, coach of a sandlot team called the Parkviews. Laurie convinced the young first baseman to pitch for him, and in one of his first games, Sandy hurled a no-hitter.

Sandy's pitching surprised family members, who thought of him more as a basketball player than as a baseball player. But as Sandy's success on the mound increased, so did his love for baseball. Word of his fastball began to spread, and scouts started appearing whenever the youngster was scheduled to pitch.

Sandy planned on going to college rather than signing with a professional team. His parents had always stressed the importance of a college education, and the lesson had taken hold. Eventually, he wanted to become an architect. He told all the baseball scouts that he would not sign a pro contract unless he received a bonus that was large enough to cover his college costs in the event he did not make it to the major leagues.

He applied to the University of Cincinnati and was awarded a basketball scholarship in 1953. Cincinnati was not known as a baseball powerhouse, but the university's basketball team, led by all-American Jack Twyman, was very good. In fact, starting in 1958, Cincinnati made it to the Final Four five straight times, and in 1961 and 1962 they were the NCAA national champions.

In the fall of 1953, Koufax packed his baseball cleats and his basketball shoes and headed west. Baseball took a back seat as he averaged more than 20 points a game and helped lead the freshman basketball squad to a 12–2 season under coach Ed Jucker.

Coincidentally, Jucker was also the university's varsity baseball coach. Sandy started several games in the spring of 1954 and experienced a good deal of success. He fashioned a winning 3–1 record, striking out 51 batters in just 31 innings. But he showed that he still needed a great deal of work on his control as he walked 30 batters.

During this time, many major-league teams continued to show an interest in him, especially the Dodgers, the Milwaukee Braves, and the Pittsburgh Pirates. Sandy greatly impressed Dodgers head scout Al Campanis during a tryout with Brooklyn. "I'll always remember that first pitch," Campanis said later. "It was a fastball that looked like it would hit the dirt in front of the plate. Then, all of a sudden, it rose for a kneehigh strike. As soon as I saw that fastball, the hair raised up on my arms."

Brooklyn made an offer that Sandy and his father found acceptable, and the contract was signed in December 1954. Sandy would leave the University of Cincinnati but continue his education during the winter at Columbia University.

In an attempt to cut down on the amount of money being spent on young prospects, the major leagues had instituted a "bonus rule." The rule stated that if a team awarded a bonus of more than $4,000 to a player, it had to keep him on its big-league roster for two years. The team would thus have to give a spot on its roster to a young player rather than to a seasoned professional who might help the club win more games. Sandy's contract called for a salary of $6,000 a year for both 1955 and 1956 plus a $14,000 signing bonus.

As a "bonus baby" at the tender age of 19, Sandy Koufax would be starting his professional baseball career not in the minor leagues but with the hometown Brooklyn Dodgers. Incredibly, he had not yet pitched 20 games in his entire life.

3

THE
BONUS BABY

When Sandy Koufax arrived at the Dodgers' training camp complex in Vero Beach, Florida, in the spring of 1955, he was given uniform number 32. Joe Becker, the new Dodgers pitching coach, took the 19-year-old Koufax under his wing and made him his special project. Running and more running became the order of the day as Koufax began to get himself into shape for his first season as a major leaguer.

The Brooklyn Dodgers had finished in second place in 1954, five games behind the pennant-winning New York Giants. Their roster was sprinkled with future Hall of Famers such as Jackie Robinson, Pee Wee Reese, Roy Campanella, and Duke Snider, as well as Gil Hodges, Carl Furillo, Jim Gilliam, Don Newcombe, and Carl Erskine.

The team got off to a fast start in 1955, winning its first 10 games and 12 of its next 14. But they did it without Koufax. Relegated to the bench, the rookie southpaw got to watch just one game before being placed on the 30-day disabled list. He had suffered a hairline fracture of his ankle when he had stepped on a sprinkler head

Koufax holds up the game ball after his 14-strikeout victory against the Cincinnati Reds on August 27, 1955. The 14 whiffs was the highest in the N.L. that year, and his two wins were shutouts.

during his pregame run. By the time he returned to the active roster, it was already June and the Dodgers were well on their way to the National League pennant.

It was not until June 24, in Brooklyn's 66th game of the year, that Koufax finally made his long-delayed big-league debut. With the Dodgers trailing the Milwaukee Braves, 5–1, manager Walter Alston brought him in to pitch the 5th inning of a night game in Milwaukee's County Stadium.

Koufax's first few throws were hardly the stuff a manager dreams of. After surrendering a bloop hit to leadoff hitter Johnny Logan, Koufax made a wild throw on a bunt attempt by Eddie Mathews and walked Henry Aaron to load the bases with none out. But then he reached back for something extra and fanned Bobby Thomson on a blazing fastball: one out. The next batter,

Warming up in Ebbets Field, Koufax displays the easy motion that made him one of the most feared pitchers in N.L. history. "Trying to hit Koufax," Pirate slugger Willie Stargell observed in 1972, "was like trying to drink coffee with a fork."

slugging first baseman Joe Adcock, grounded into a double play to retire the side, and Koufax got out of the inning without allowing a run.

Following a similar relief appearance against the New York Giants (Koufax again loaded the bases with none out but did not give up a run), he was rewarded with his first major league start on July 6 against the Pittsburgh Pirates. This time he surrendered 3 hits and 1 run in $4\frac{2}{3}$ innings of work. He also walked 8 batters while striking out 4.

The Dodgers slumped for a while, and Koufax was limited to just 3 brief relief appearances over the next 50 days. When the time came for his next start, however, he was ready for it.

The powerful Cincinnati Reds were the Dodgers' opponents that day, and Koufax's family and friends were in the stands to cheer him on. The Reds managed just two hits against Koufax—

During his first three years with the Dodgers, Koufax had the benefit of pitching to veteran Roy Campanella (left), one of the greatest catchers in baseball history. A tragic auto accident in January 1958 left Campy permanently injured.

one in the first inning and another in the 9th. With an exploding fastball, Koufax finished up with a brilliant 7–0 shutout, striking out 14 batters while walking 5.

Unfortunately, the emotional high from the game did not last long. Less than a week later, Koufax was bombed by the Braves in a one-inning relief appearance. Three days after that, he was given another start and repeated his success of the previous week. He allowed just 5 hits to the Pittsburgh Pirates, winning 4–0 for his second complete-game shutout. And this time he walked only 2 while striking out 6.

The Dodgers clinched the pennant soon afterward, and Koufax saw limited action the rest of the season as the team concentrated on preparing for the World Series. He made only three more appearances, losing twice, to even his record at 2–2. His ERA in 12 games was a respectable 3.02, and he allowed just 33 hits in 41²/₃ innings of work, striking out 30 and walking 28.

The Dodgers went on to defeat the New York Yankees in the World Series, with Johnny Podres hurling a 2–0 shutout in the decisive seventh game. After many years of disappointment and countless cries of "Wait 'til next year"—the Dodgers had played in seven World Series but had never come out on top—Brooklyn finally had a championship team to call its own.

Even though he did not appear in the Fall Classic, Koufax received a check for $9,768.21— nearly $4,000 more than his salary—as his share for being a member of the winning club. The future looked bright indeed for the young lefty.

4

HARNESSING THE TALENT

Koufax reported to Vero Beach in the spring of 1956 intent on contributing even more to the Dodger cause. When the regular season began, however, he found himself in a difficult position. In order to improve, he needed more experience in game situations. But with the Dodgers once more contending for a pennant, they could not afford to use anyone but their most consistent, proven players.

As a result, Koufax did not progress as fast as he had hoped he would. Due to the bonus rule, he had to be kept on the big-league roster and could not be farmed out to the minors, where he would have had a chance to pitch regularly. Instead, he appeared in only 16 games and pitched just 58 2/3 innings in 1956. With so few chances, it was natural that the young pitcher

Between innings of a game on August 25, 1957 in historic Ebbets Field, Koufax (left) and Sal Maglie warm up in the Brooklyn bullpen. Rightfielder Gino Cimoli throws a ball in front of the scoreboard, at the base of which is sign for Abe Stark's clothing store. Any player who hit a ball off the sign won a free suit of clothes.

would try too hard to impress management the few times he took the mound.

"I missed that training, that experience a young pitcher needs," he said later. "A couple of seasons in the minor leagues would probably have solved my control problem, and I might have been ready to win in the National League three or four years before I finally found myself."

Despite his lack of activity, Koufax's big-league education continued. Veteran pitcher Sal Maglie came over to Brooklyn from the Cleveland Indians early in the season and helped teach the youngster how to set up batters and think along with them. In addition, Maglie gave the team a needed boost that helped carry the Dodgers all the way to another National League pennant.

Their World Series opponents were once again the Yankees, but that year the Bronx Bombers were not to be denied. In a Series highlighted by Don Larsen's perfect game, the New Yorkers edged out Brooklyn, four games to three.

After the season, Koufax felt he needed more work on his pitching and elected to play in the Puerto Rican winter league. He got some much-needed experience playing for Caguas, then reported to spring training with the Dodgers.

Koufax had spent a month on the disabled list in 1955, so the two years he was required to stay on the major-league roster would not be up until 30 days into the 1957 season. He had one month left to prove he belonged in the big leagues. On that final day, May 16, Koufax was scheduled to start against the Chicago Cubs.

As luck would have it, he proceeded to dominate the Cubs, striking out 14 batters en route to a 3–2, complete-game victory. Manager Alston was so impressed that he decided to put Koufax into the starting rotation rather than farm him out to the minors for more seasoning.

Inconsistency was still Koufax's downfall. Although he reached double figures in strikeouts in three more games that year, he won only once after June 4. He finished the year with a mediocre 5–4 record, which mirrored the Dodgers' play that year. The team dropped to third place, 11 games behind the pennant-winning Milwaukee Braves.

Around then, Dodgers president Walter O'Malley announced that the franchise would be moving to Los Angeles, California, the following year. The tradition of National League baseball in Brooklyn, which had begun in 1890, was coming to an end, and the Brooklyn-born Koufax felt the uprooting more than many of the other players.

The final game played by the Brooklyn Dodgers was against the Phillies in Philadelphia. With his team down, 2–1, after 7 1/2 innings, Koufax was called in from the bullpen to pitch the bottom of the 8th inning. He allowed 2 walks but no hits or runs and fanned third baseman Willie Jones for the last out. When the Dodgers failed to score in the 9th, Sandy Koufax went down in the record books as the final hurler to throw a pitch for the Brooklyn Dodgers.

But before moving to the West Coast, Koufax had another appointment to keep. Along with teammate Don Drysdale, he spent the winter fulfilling his military obligation at Fort Dix in New Jersey.

Koufax's 1960 Topps bubblegum card.

5

A NEW START

Sandy Koufax and Don Drysdale joined the Dodgers in time for the beginning of the 1958 season, but it was not a happy reunion. Roy Campanella, the team's All-Star catcher, had been seriously injured in an automobile accident that January. He would be confined to a wheelchair for the rest of his life.

Meanwhile, the rest of the Dodgers had to get used to their new ballpark. In Brooklyn, they had played at cozy Ebbets Field, a stadium ideally suited to the team because the distance from home plate to the outfield fences was not very far. The club had consistently been among the league leaders in home runs, as sluggers such as Campanella, Duke Snider, Gil Hodges, and Carl Furillo took full advantage of the ballpark's small dimensions.

During their first year in California, however, the Dodgers' home field was the Los Angeles Coliseum. Originally built for the 1932 Olympic Games, the stadium was much better suited for football than for baseball. The left-field fence was only 251 feet from home plate, and a 42-foot-high screen had been erected above the

Pitching in mammoth L.A. Coliseum on September 6, 1959, Koufax strikes out the Cubs' Cal Neeman to run his strikeout total to 41 in three games, breaking his own N.L. record.

fence in an attempt to cut down on cheap home runs. Right field and right center, however, were cavernous. Many of the Dodgers were so affected by the stadium that they failed to match their previous years' production.

For Koufax, the season began just as his Brooklyn seasons had. He did not pitch regularly until May 20, when he hurled an 11-inning victory over Milwaukee for his first win of the campaign. Things started looking up after that, and by July he had a respectable 7–3 mark, even though the Dodgers as a team were floundering.

His next start, however, proved costly. While covering first base on a play against the Cubs, Koufax injured his ankle and was sidelined for two weeks. He never got back into a groove after returning and lost 8 of his final 12 decisions. When put into the context of a seventh-place team that finished 12 games below .500 and 21 games out of first, his 11–11 record was fairly respectable. But Koufax was far from satisfied.

Unfortunately, the 1959 season started out much like the previous one. Koufax struggled early in the year and seemed on the verge of being demoted.

"He has no coordination and he has lost all his confidence," said pitching coach Joe Becker. "His arm is sound, but mechanically he is all fouled up."

Koufax finally won his first game of the year on the last day of May, then went on to take his next four decisions. "He's either awfully good or awfully bad," said manager Walter Alston.

One of Koufax's wins was a 6–2 victory over the Phillies on June 22. He fanned 16 batters in the contest to set a major-league record for strikeouts in a night game. The record lasted just a little more than two months, then it was broken by the man who had set it.

On the night of August 31, exactly a week after striking out 13 Phillies in an 8–2 win, Koufax took the mound against the Giants in a tense battle for first place. Getting stronger as the game progressed, he struck out 15 batters over the last 6 innings, giving him a total of 18 for the game and tying Bob Feller's all-time single-game mark. More than 82,000 people, the largest crowd of the year, witnessed the incredible performance. Koufax also set a new major-league mark for most strikeouts in two successive games (31).

Koufax did not win another game after his victory over the Giants. The Dodgers, however, continued their winning ways. Los Angeles moved into first place two days before the end of the season, then finished in a tie with the Braves.

Dodger manager Walter Alston (right) greets his two young pitching aces Don Drysdale (left) and Koufax in the spring of 1958. Drysdale played 14 years under Alston, the longest career in the majors under a single manager.

A best-of-three playoff ensued, with the Dodgers taking the opener, 3–2, in a cold drizzle in Milwaukee. Larry Sherry pitched 7⅔ innings of scoreless relief for the win. In the second game, Los Angeles overcame a 5–2 deficit to tie the score in the 9th and went on to win it, 6–5, in the 12th. By doing so, they completed one of the most remarkable turnarounds in big-league history, going from seventh place to first in a single season.

The 1959 World Series pitted the Dodgers against the Chicago White Sox. The Sox trounced five Dodgers pitchers for an 11–0 shutout in the opener, but the Dodgers bounced back to win games 2, 3, and 4. Having hurled two scoreless innings of relief in the first game, Sandy was rewarded with his first Series start in game 5.

A record crowd of more than 92,000 filled the Coliseum in anticipation of seeing the home team capture its first title on the West Coast. Koufax allowed only one run in seven innings, but the Dodgers could not score at all off three Chicago pitchers and lost the game, 1–0. The Series ended two days later, with a 9–3 Dodgers victory in Chicago.

For the second time, Sandy Koufax was a member of a world championship club. Yet his career mark after five big-league seasons was just one game over .500. And his most frustrating year of all was yet to come.

The 1960 season saw Koufax get off to his worst start ever. Things got so bad that, after one brief relief appearance, he suggested to Dodgers general manager Buzzie Bavasi that a change in scenery might be best for all parties concerned.

"Buzzie," Koufax said, "why don't you trade me? I want to pitch, and I'm not going to get a chance here."

"How can we pitch you," Bavasi replied, "when you can't get anyone out?"

By the middle of June, Koufax's record was a dismal 1–8, his only victory coming on a one-hit shutout over the Pirates. Even when he pitched well, he still came up short. Twice he struck out 15 batters in a game, yet both times he lost. He eventually managed to win five games in a row, but then he lost his next four starts.

Koufax finished the year with an 8–13 record for a Dodgers club that dropped to fourth place in the National League standings. On the positive side, his ERA (3.91) fell below 4.00 for the first time since 1957, and he finished second in the league in strikeouts. Teammate Don Drysdale was first.

Still, after six years in the majors, Koufax was beginning to wonder if he would ever fulfill his tremendous potential. He had finally gotten the chance to pitch regularly, but control problems continued to plague him throughout the 1960 season. For the second time in his career, he had walked at least 100 batters in a season.

That fall and winter, Koufax gave serious thought to his future plans. He contemplated life without baseball and went so far as to enter into a business partnership as a manufacturer's representative. Having been involved in sports all his life, however, Koufax found it was not easy to turn his back and walk away from the playing field. After another period of self-examination, he decided to give himself one more year in which to succeed.

Sandy Koufax was determined to do every-thing in his power to prepare himself for the 1961 season. He reported to spring training in the best shape of his life. His informal chat with Norm Sherry on the plane ride to Orlando rein-forced the basic pitching principles he had been taught over the years, and the success achieved that day convinced him that he was at last headed in the right direction.

Following a loss in his first game of the regular season, Koufax won 3 in a row and 9 of his next 10 decisions. Included were six con-secutive complete-game victories from May 21 through June 11. His first-half work earned him his first berth on the National League All-Star team.

Koufax's performance fell off after the break. Still, he won 18 games for the second-place Dodgers and broke Christy Mathewson's N.L. single-season strikeout mark in the process by fanning 269 batters. His 15 complete games more than doubled his previous high, and his ERA dropped to 3.52.

The background scoreboard tells the story on May 11, 1963: Two outs, 9th inning, and the Giants with no hits. Koufax walked Willie McCov-ey but got the last out for a no-hitter.

Koufax's final victory of the season took on added historical significance: It was the last game ever played in the Los Angeles Coliseum. The Dodgers would be moving into Dodger Stadium, their luxurious new park in Chavez Ravine, in 1962.

Koufax was superb that September day in 1961, going all the way in a 13-inning, 3–2 victory over the Chicago Cubs. He fanned 15 batters—the 11th time that year he reached double figures in strikeouts—for his season high.

Koufax had made the transition that escapes so many young hurlers. He had gone from being a thrower to being a pitcher. He used both his blazing fastball and sharp-breaking curveball to perfection. No longer did he attempt to overpower opposing hitters with every pitch. He went to the mound with a simple plan in mind: Get ahead of the batter in the count, then make him hit the pitch you want him to hit. "I became a good pitcher," Koufax said later, "when I stopped trying to make them miss the ball and started trying to make them hit it."

The Dodgers moved to Chavez Ravine in 1962 as scheduled. That same year, National League baseball returned to Koufax's hometown with a new expansion team, the New York Mets. As the fumbling, bumbling Mets struggled to be taken seriously in the big leagues, Koufax was having his own ups and downs. Although he would have some great moments that season—striking out 18 batters in a game for the second time in his career, as well as hurling the first of his four no-hitters—he also began to have some disturbing circulation problems in the index finger of his throwing hand.

The first sign of trouble came in mid-May,

when he started to experience numbness in the finger. Although it did not get better, it did not seem to affect his pitching, either. In fact, a month and a half later, on June 30, he fanned 13 Mets batters in the no-hitter while running his record to 11–4. This momentous occasion was greeted with a smile by some skeptics. It was not quite the same as if he had no-hit a real major-league team, they scoffed. The Mets were, after all, in the midst of losing a modern-record 120 games in their maiden season.

The finger got worse, and by the middle of the season it was a reddish-blue color. Koufax knew something would have to be done about it. Dodgers team physician Robert Kerlan suggested he see a cardiovascular specialist.

Tests showed that circulation in the finger was only 15 percent of what it should have been.

The doctors were not sure whether Koufax's problem was the result of a blood clot caused by a bruise, or Raynaud's phenomenon, a rare and incurable disease. Nevertheless, a specialist, Dr. Travis Winsor, started the finger on the road to recovery by treating it with four different drugs, and several weeks later the problem seemed to have cleared up.

"You're very lucky," Dr. Kerlan told Koufax. "You don't know how close you came to losing the finger."

Koufax returned to action after a layoff of two months, only to be knocked out in the first inning of his first start. The Dodgers were on top of the National League standings at the time, but Koufax's performance was an omen of things to

In July 1962, Dr. Robert Wood examined Koufax's numbed and swollen finger. In the eight games he pitched after the finger went dead, he gave up four runs and struck out 77 in 67 1/3 innings.

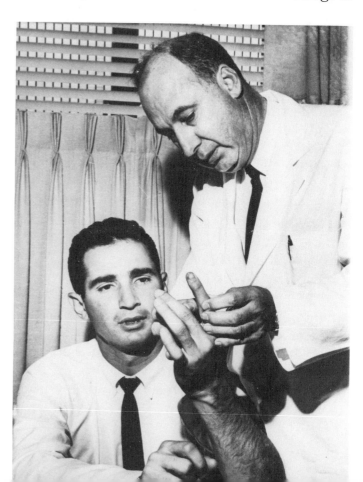

come. They lost seven of their last eight regular-season games and finished tied for first place with the San Francisco Giants. For the second time in four years, a best-of-three-games playoff would decide the National League pennant. The Giants won the first game, 8–0, as veteran pitcher Billy Pierce won his 12th straight game at Candlestick Park. The Dodgers came back to win the second playoff game. A crowd of 45,693 turned out for the deciding game. The Dodgers took a lead into the 9th inning, only to see the Giants score four runs and win, 6–4, for the right to face the Yankees in the World Series.

Although Koufax again finished second to Drysdale in strikeouts, and his 2.54 earned run average was the best in the league, it was a disappointing season for him as well as for the Dodgers. After defeating the New York Mets on July 12, Koufax's record had been 14–4. He did not win a game after that date and finished the year at 14–7.

Dodger hopes were high for 1963, however. Unlike their previous home fields, Dodger Stadium in Chavez Ravine was a pitcher's park, and the makeup of the team was changing to take advantage of this fact, especially as the old guard of Snider, Hodges, and Furillo began to leave the club. Tommy Davis and Frank Howard were around to bolster the hitting, but shortstop Maury Wills was now the team's catalyst. In 1962, he had stolen a record 104 bases to lead the major leagues.

The 1963 season was a textbook example of what can be accomplished by a team that combines great pitching with excellent speed and timely hitting. The Dodgers won the pennant by six games over the St. Louis Cardinals. Their pitching staff dominated the league, and Sandy Koufax was the leader of them all. His accomplishments included the following: an outstanding 1.88 ERA to lead the N.L. for the second year in a row; 25 victories to tie Juan Marichal of the Giants for the league lead; 306 strikeouts to break his own single-season league mark; and 11 shutouts to set an all-time major-league mark for lefthanders (he had hurled only 9 shutouts during his first 8 seasons).

On May 11, Koufax faced Juan Marichal and the first-place Giants at Dodger Stadium. Koufax struck out just four and walked two batters, but he gave up no hits and thus fashioned his second career no-hitter. "It's too bad I walked those two guys," an elated Koufax said afterward, "but it is still my greatest thrill."

The Dodgers' reward for their second West Coast pennant was a chance to meet the Yankees in the World Series. Their old rivals had just won their fourth straight pennant and were looking to win their third Series in a row. Koufax and the Dodgers, however, had other plans.

The Yankees opened the Series with Whitey Ford, their ace. It would not be easy for Koufax to top Ford, but he did. Koufax struck out the first five Yankee batters he faced, and after he had been staked to a 4–0 lead his fastball was still humming. He struck out 15 batters in the game to break a World Series mark set by his former teammate, Carl Erskine.

After the game, Yankees catcher Yogi Berra commented: "I can see how he won twenty-five games. What I don't understand is how he lost five."

Veteran Johnny Podres, who had beaten the Yankees twice in the 1955 World Series, then

took the mound and whipped the Yankees, 4–1, to send the series to Los Angeles.

Game 3 featured the Yankees' 21-game winner Jim Bouton against Don Drysdale, who had struggled to a 19–17 record during the season. But on this day Drysdale looked like his old self and won, 1–0. The Dodgers were ahead 3–0 with Koufax and Ford ready to duel again.

Ford was superb in game 4, allowing the Dodgers just two hits. The first hit was Frank Howard's home run in the 5th inning to give the Dodgers a 1–0 lead. Then Mickey Mantle, struggling with just one hit in the three previous games, timed a Koufax curveball perfectly and slashed it into the center-field bleachers for a homer to tie the game. In the bottom of the seventh inning, a three-base error by Joe Pepitone allowed Jim Gilliam to reach third base for the Dodgers. A long line sacrifice fly by Willie Davis

As the last putout was made in game 4 of the 1963 World Series, Koufax and the Los Angeles fans celebrate the Dodgers' 4-game sweep. It was the first time the mighty Yankees had been swept in 28 World Series appearances.

brought Gilliam home for the go-ahead run. Koufax held on, giving up just six hits, and the Dodgers won, 2–1. By beating Whitey Ford for the second time in six days, Koufax had given the Dodgers a sweep of the mighty Yankees.

Few people knew that Koufax had been pitching the last few weeks under great emotional stress. His father had suffered a heart attack prior to the end of the regular season, and thoughts of him weighed heavily on the pitcher's mind. The Series clincher turned out to be doubly sweet, as his father had just been released from the hospital.

For his overall performance against the Yankees, Koufax was chosen the Most Valuable Player of the World Series and received a brand-new Corvette from *Sport* magazine in recognition of the achievement. Shortly thereafter, he com-

Koufax holds up the jewel-encrusted Hickock belt, awarded to him for being the top professional Athlete in 1963. Koufax won the Cy Young and MVP Awards that year as well.

pleted a sweep of the most prestigious honors given to a pitcher. He was named the Most Valuable Player of the National League and won the Cy Young Award, which was then given to just one pitcher in the major leagues. He was named as baseball's best hurler on every ballot, the first time in the seven years of the Cy Young Award that there had been a unanimous winner.

But even that honor was not enough to express some people's admiration. Los Angeles civil service commissioner Ike Greenberg went so far as to propose that the city change the name of Fairfax Avenue to Koufax Avenue.

THE ARTFUL DODGER

S andy Koufax began the 1964 season by pitching the Opening Day game for the first time in his career. He was more than up to the task as he defeated the St. Louis Cardinals with a six-hit shutout. A minor flaw in his pitching mechanics caused him some problems over the first part of the season, however, and his record was only 4–4 at the end of May.

Together with Coach Becker, Koufax finally figured out what he was doing wrong. To say that he made an adjustment and corrected the mistake is putting it mildly. He proceeded to win 11 games in a row. Included in the streak was the third no-hitter of his career, tying him with Larry Corcoran, Cy Young, and Bob Feller for the most ever by a pitcher. The victims on June 4 were the first-place Philadelphia Phillies.

Koufax struck out 12 in the game and said afterward of his pitching, "I have been studying pictures in magazines of my form and suddenly realized that I had been stepping too far to my left with the right foot across my body, sort of blocking myself. Tonight in the first few innings I concentrated on making an adjustment. It felt fine."

An injury to his elbow cut short Koufax's season in the middle of August. Dr. Kerlan had the swollen joint X-rayed, and the tests showed that an arthritic change had taken place due to the thousands upon thousands of pitches thrown over the years. Koufax was informed that the condition, caused by excessive wear and tear on the body, could be controlled but not cured. The swelling and soreness would come and go every time he threw.

"I could see it blow up," Koufax said of his elbow when he tried to move it. "It sounded as if I were squeezing a soggy sponge."

The best plan seemed to be to give the arm complete rest for the remainder of the year and hope for the best in 1965.

Koufax's final statistics for 1964 showed a 19–5 record and a league-leading ERA of 1.74. These marks were not enough to salvage the season for Los Angeles, however. The Dodgers finished 13 games behind the pennant-winning St. Louis Cardinals, in sixth place, and Koufax went home to ponder his uncertain future.

The next spring, the elbow continued to swell up, but cortisone shots administered directly into the joint seemed to help. Koufax's arthritis received a great deal of attention from the media, but, surprisingly, the act of pitching itself seemed to lessen the effects of the condition. Koufax never needed another cortisone shot once the 1965 season began. Swelling and soreness were his constant companions during the season, but the pain was usually gone by the time he loosened up and began to pitch in a game. A postgame ice treatment for his arm became a regular practice.

Despite the pain, Koufax managed not only to pitch regularly in 1965 but to pitch incredibly well. He led the National League in wins (26), winning percentage (.765), earned run average (2.04), complete games (27), and innings pitched (335.2). His 382 strikeouts set a new major-league mark as well. In addition, he hurled 8 shutouts, fanned 10 or more in 21 games, and was the starting and winning pitcher in the All-Star Game.

Surprisingly, Koufax seemed to pitch some of his best games with only two days' rest. "When you get too much rest," he wrote, "your arm seems strong at the beginning, but your control tends to be haphazard, and the bottom falls out on you in the middle of the game."

The highlight of Koufax's 1965 season was a

In game 5 of the 1965 World Series, Koufax swings a bat and talks with shortstop Maury Wills. Koufax then poked an RBI-single for his only hit in 19 World Series at bats. Wills had four hits to back Sandy's four-hit shutout.

September 9 contest against the Chicago Cubs. That night, he became the first pitcher in history to hurl a fourth no-hitter and, also, just the ninth pitcher to toss a perfect game. The game was one of the great pitching duels of all time, as opposing hurler Bob Hendley of Chicago allowed just one hit: a bloop double by Lou Johnson, who was the only player to reach base during the game. The lone run scored when Johnson walked, was sacrificed to second base, stole third, and scored on a wild throw by the catcher.

Hendley was tough, but the Cubs did not stand a chance against Koufax that night. Chicago infielder Joe Amalfitano, who later became a Dodgers coach, struck out for the 26th out. "Harvey Kuenn was on deck," he recalled. "I told him, 'Watch out, Harv. He's really humming.' Harvey said, 'Wait here, Joe. I'll be right back.' He went down on three pitches, too." Coincidentally, Amalfitano and Kuenn had been with the Giants in 1963 when Koufax threw his second no-hitter: In that game, Amalfitano had led off the 9th inning, and Kuenn had made the last out. Koufax struck out 14 against the Cubs, and Kuenn's whiff in the 9th was the Dodger hurler's 6th in a row.

Los Angeles went on to win the pennant by a two-game margin over the Giants. The pennant was clinched on the second-to-last day of the season, when Koufax set down the Braves, 3–1, just three days after hurling a two-hit shutout against Cincinnati. He fanned 13 batters in each contest.

The weak-hitting Dodgers (seventh in the league in batting average, eighth in runs scored, and tenth in home runs) then traveled to Minnesota to take on the hard-hitting Twins in the Fall

Classic. The Series was set to open on Yom Kippur, the holiest of Jewish holidays. Because Koufax was unable to pitch in the opener because of his religious beliefs, Don Drysdale was named to start game 1. The Twins defeated him, then bested Koufax in game 2, but the Dodgers came back and won the next two games to even the Series.

Koufax hurled a brilliant 7–0 shutout in game 5, limiting the powerful Twins to 4 harmless singles while striking out 10. But when the Series moved back to Minnesota, the Twins came through with another victory, forcing a seventh game.

It was not until he arrived at the ballpark the day of the finale that Koufax learned he would be the starting pitcher. Working again on only two days' rest, he pitched another shutout, winning 2–0. For the second time in three years, the Dodgers were World Champions.

Koufax had compiled an awesome 0.38 earned run average for the Series, surrendering just 13 hits in 24 innings to the hottest-hitting team in the American League. He walked only 5 batters and struck out 29.

For his heroics, Sandy Koufax was named the Most Valuable Player of the World Series for the second time in his career. A second unanimous Cy Young Award as the major leagues' best pitcher followed soon afterward. To top it off, he was later awarded the Hickock Belt as 1965's Professional Athlete of the Year. Having won it previously in 1963, Koufax became the first athlete to be twice honored with the prestigious award.

GOING OUT ON TOP

During Sandy Koufax's career, baseball's salary structure was kept in line by means of the reserve clause, a rule the players later challenged successfully. According to the reserve clause, a player belonged to the team that had signed him and could not move to another club on his own. Even if he chose not to re-sign with his team, it continued to own the rights to his services.

Clubs, therefore, often adopted a "take it or leave it" approach when it came to negotiating contracts. After all, if a player did not care for the terms offered, there was little he could do about it.

Koufax was not happy with his $80,000 salary for the 1965 season. There had been some ill feeling between him and the Dodgers' front office over the way negotiations had been handled back in 1964. So when it was time to sign for 1966, Koufax and Drysdale agreed to join forces in their negotiations with management. In an

A tearful Koufax, 30, announces his retirement in 1966. No pitcher in major-league history had a better final season than Koufax's 27–9 in 1966.

unprecedented action, they informed the Dodgers that neither would sign a contract unless the other was also satisfied. They asked Koufax's lawyer, Bill Hayes, to represent them in the negotiations. This also violated tradition; then, the use of an agent was unheard of.

The Dodgers were one of the most profitable franchises in all of sports. In 1965 they had drawn more than 2½ million fans to Dodger Stadium, the third-highest attendance total in

Although he had the ability to strike out many batters, Koufax said, "I became a good pitcher when I stopped trying to make them miss the ball and started trying to make them hit it."

baseball history up to that time. Koufax and Drysdale had combined for 49 of the team's 97 wins in the regular season as well as 3 of 4 World Series victories.

When the Dodgers offered Koufax $100,000 and Drysdale $85,000 for the 1966 season, the pair refused to sign. Instead, they demanded three-year contracts worth a total of $1 million, to be divided evenly between them.

The holdout lasted through spring training as the Dodgers refused to negotiate and the two pitchers refused to compromise the principles they believed in.

"I don't think Koufax and Drysdale will play for the Dodgers in '66," said Buzzie Bavasi.

"I think he's right," countered Drysdale, "because we are not accepting the Dodgers' current offer."

In the meantime, the Dynamic Duo signed contracts with Paramount Studios to appear in a movie entitled *Warning Shot* should they not be playing ball.

Shortly before the Dodgers broke camp to head north for the regular season, Bavasi contacted Koufax and Drysdale. Within a day's time, an agreement was reached, and the Dodgers were assured of their services for another year. According to Bavasi, the contracts called for Koufax to be paid $125,000 and Drysdale $110,000. They thus became the two highest-paid players in baseball, having won the largest raises in history up to that point.

In terms of today's dollars, however, Koufax's contract would be a bargain. Even taking inflation into account, it would work out to approximately $550,000 at a time when the $5-million-a-year barrier has already been broken.

Missing 32 days of spring training did not seem to hurt Koufax at all. He went on to lead the league in victories (with a career-high 27), ERA (a career-low 1.73), games started (41) and completed (27), innings pitched (323), and strikeouts (317), while tying for the lead in shutouts (5) and finishing second in winning percentage (.750).

The high point of the season for Koufax came in the final game of 1966. The Dodgers needed a victory over the Philadelphia Phillies to clinch the pennant. Pitching on two days' rest, Koufax led, 6–0, going into the bottom of the 9th inning. Although Philadelphia then scored three runs, the Dodger ace held on for the win. For the third time in four years, the Dodgers would be playing in the World Series.

After the grueling pennant race, Los Angeles proved to be no match for the American League champion Baltimore Orioles. In game 1, the Orioles scored three times against Drysdale in the top half of the first inning. That turned out to be one run more than the Dodgers would score in the entire Series.

Baltimore swept Los Angeles in four games, winning by scores of 5–2, 6–0, 1–0, and 1–0. Koufax allowed just one earned run in six innings in game 2 but suffered defeat at the hands of Jim Palmer, who became the youngest pitcher in World Series history to hurl a complete-game shutout.

A little more than one month later, on November 18, Sandy Koufax shocked the entire sports world by announcing his retirement from baseball. He was only 30 years old.

In a sport in which players often hang on way past their prime (mostly to continue receiving large paychecks), the idea of someone retiring at

Koufax is an excellent golfer and since retiring plays often. When a golf pro told him to keep his arm straight while swinging the club, Koufax answered, "If I could straighten it out, I'd be pitching at Dodger Stadium tonight."

the very top of his game was hard for many to comprehend. But Koufax had made up his mind. Even more than the physical pain he had to endure each time he threw, the deciding factor in Koufax's decision was his doctors' prognosis: If Koufax continued to pitch, his arm would likely be crippled.

The Dodgers reportedly tried to lure him back for the 1967 season with a salary offer of $150,000, but Koufax held firm. It was not a question of money for him but one of health. Ironically, had Koufax been pitching today, his elbow condition could have been corrected and his career extended for many more years.

"I had a bunch of spurs in there," Koufax later explained, "but they didn't want to operate. . . . I don't know how much longer I could have pitched, but today I could have had surgery over the winter and been back the next season."

Still, Koufax had no regrets. "I wasn't bitter about having to retire," he said. "Some guys spend their entire lives in the minor leagues trying to make the majors, and I had 12 years. I was very fortunate."

Following his exit as an active player, Koufax worked as an NBC sports commentator for three years. Considered one of the most eligible bachelors of the 1960s, he married Anne Widmark, daughter of actor Richard Widmark, and moved to Maine.

In 1979, Koufax rejoined the Dodgers as a roving minor-league pitching instructor, a position he enjoyed for more than a decade. "Teaching is fun," he said at the time. "I enjoy it. These players are on their way up, and they've all got their dreams. It's a very positive thing."

Although he rarely appears on television or at baseball memorabilia shows, Sandy Koufax did make one special public appearance in 1972. That year he appeared in Cooperstown, New York, where he was inducted into the Baseball Hall of Fame. At age 36, he became the youngest player ever elected, gathering more votes than anyone else had ever received in the 40-year history of the balloting.

"This is the greatest honor I've ever been given," he said, "not just in baseball, but in my life. I'm a little surprised I got as many votes as I did. I didn't have as many good years as some others in the Hall, and I thought that might count against me."

In another ceremony that same year, the Dodgers retired Koufax's uniform number, 32, putting him in the same company as a number of his former teammates from the great Dodger teams of the 1950s: Pee Wee Reese, Duke Snider, Jim Gilliam, Walt Alston, Roy Campanella, and Jackie Robinson. A few years later, Don Drysdale's number, 53, would also be retired.

Today, Koufax continues to work with the Dodgers at spring training and to spend the rest of the year out of the public eye. Even so, his graceful manner and overpowering presence on the mound are still remembered, and they will be as long as the game of baseball is played. For, as legendary manager Casey Stengel once said about Sandy Koufax, "The kid is probably the best of them all."

CHRONOLOGY

Dec. 30, 1935	Sanford Braun born in Brooklyn, New York, to Jack and Evelyn Braun
1939	The Brauns divorce
1945	Evelyn Braun marries Irving Koufax; family moves to Rockville Center, New York
1950	Family moves back to Brooklyn
Dec. 14, 1954	Signs bonus contract with Brooklyn Dodgers
June 24, 1955	Makes big-league debut against the Milwaukee Braves
Aug. 31, 1959	Strikes out 18 Giants to tie major-league record
Apr. 24, 1962	Strikes out 18 Chicago Cubs to tie major-league mark
June 30, 1962	Hurls no-hitter against the New York Mets
May 11, 1963	Hurls no-hitter against the San Francisco Giants
Oct. 2, 1963	Strikes out 15 Yankees to set new World Series record
Oct. 6, 1963	Defeats Yankees to clinch World Series
1963	Wins N.L. Most Valuable Player award, Cy Young award, World Series MVP, and the Hickock Belt
June 4, 1964	Hurls no-hitter against the Philadelphia Phillies
July 13, 1965	Is the winning pitcher in the All-Star game
Sept. 9, 1965	Hurls perfect game against the Chicago Cubs.
1965	Sets N.L. season mark with 382 strikeouts
Oct. 14, 1965	Shuts out Minnesota to clinch World Series
1965	Wins Cy Young Award, World Series MVP Award, and the Hickock Belt
Spring 1966	Stages 32-day joint holdout with Don Drysdale before signing record $125,000 contract
Oct. 2, 1966	Wins his last major league game
1966	Wins record fifth consecutive ERA title
1966	Wins Cy Young award
Nov. 18, 1966	Announces retirement from baseball
1969	Marries Anne Widmark
1970	Named Player of the Decade for the 1960s
1972	Inducted into the Baseball Hall of Fame
June 4, 1972	Uniform number (32) retired by Dodgers
1979–1990	Minor league pitching instructor with Dodgers

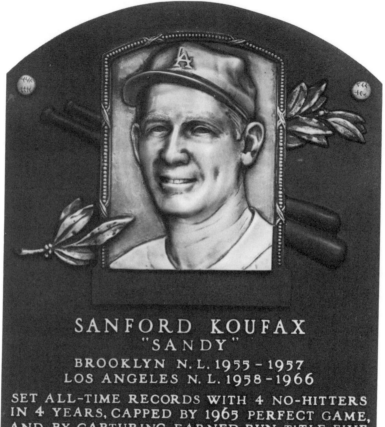

SANFORD KOUFAX
"SANDY"
BROOKLYN N.L. 1955-1957
LOS ANGELES N.L. 1958-1966

SET ALL-TIME RECORDS WITH 4 NO-HITTERS
IN 4 YEARS, CAPPED BY 1965 PERFECT GAME,
AND BY CAPTURING EARNED-RUN TITLE FIVE
SEASONS IN A ROW, 1962-1966. WON 25 OR
MORE GAMES THREE TIMES. HAD 11 SHUTOUTS
IN 1963. STRIKEOUT LEADER FOUR TIMES,
WITH RECORD 382 IN 1965. FANNED 18 IN A
GAME TWICE. MOST VALUABLE PLAYER 1963.
CY YOUNG AWARD WINNER 1963-65-66.

MAJOR LEAGUE STATISTICS

BROOKLYN DODGERS, LOS ANGELES DODGERS

YEAR	TEAM	W	L	PCT	ERA	G	GS	CG	IP	H	BB	SO	ShO
1955	BKN N	2	2	.500	3.02	12	5	2	41.2	33	28	30	2
1956		2	4	.333	4.91	16	10	0	58.2	66	29	30	0
1957		5	4	.556	3.88	34	13	2	104.1	83	54	122	0
1958	LA N	11	11	.500	4.48	40	26	5	158.2	132	105	131	0
1959		8	6	.571	4.05	35	23	6	153.1	136	92	173	1
1960		8	13	.387	3.91	37	26	7	175	133	100	197	2
1961		18	13	.581	3.52	42	35	15	255.2	212	96	269	2
1962		14	7	.667	2.54	28	26	11	184.1	134	57	216	2
1963		25	5	.833	1.88	40	40	20	311	214	58	306	11
1964		19	5	.792	1.74	29	28	15	223	154	53	223	7
1965		26	8	.765	2.04	43	41	27	335.2	216	71	382	8
1966		27	9	.750	1.73	41	41	27	323	241	77	317	5
Totals		165	87	.655	2.76	397	314	137	2324.1	1754	817	2396	40
World Series (4 years)		4	3	.571	0.95	8	7	4	57	36	11	61	2
All-Star Games (3 years)		1	0	.000	0.00	4	-	-	6	4	2	3	-

FURTHER READING

Borst, Bill. *A Fan's Memoir.* St. Louis: Krank Press, 1982.

Holmes, Tommy. *The Dodgers.* New York: Rutledge Books, 1975.

Karst, Gene, and Martin J. Jones Jr. *Who's Who in Professional Baseball.* New Rochelle, NY: Arlington House, 1973.

Kerrane, Kevin. *The Hurlers.* Alexandria, VA: Redefinition, 1989.

Koufax, Sandy, with Ed Linn. *Koufax.* New York: Viking Press, 1966.

Mitchell, Jerry. *Sandy Koufax.* New York: Grosset & Dunlap, 1966.

Okrent, Daniel, and Harris Lewine, eds. *The Ultimate Baseball Book.* Boston: Houghton Mifflin, 1979.

Thorn, John, and John B. Holway. *The Pitcher.* New York: Prentice-Hall, 1987.

Tiemann, Robert L. *Dodger Classics.* St. Louis: Baseball Histories, 1983.

Whittingham, Richard. *The Los Angeles Dodgers.* New York: HarperCollins, 1982.

INDEX

Page numbers in italics refer to illustrations.

PICTURE CREDITS

AP/Wide World Photos: pp. 12, 37, 38, 44, 50, 58; National Baseball Library, Cooperstown, NY: pp. 34, 55, 60; Princeton Desktop
Publishing: p. 24; The Sporting News: p. 52; Copyright The Topps Company, Inc.: p. 27; University of Cincinnati: p. 15; UPI/
Bettmann: pp. 2, 8, 18, 20, 21, 22, 28, 41, 42, 47

JOHN F. GRABOWSKI was educated at the City College of New York, where he was a member of the baseball team, and at Teachers College, Columbia University, where he received his master's in educational psychology. He currently teaches high school math and computer studies on Staten Island. He is a free-lance writer who has had several hundred pieces published in newspapers, magazines, and the programs of professional teams. The author of *Super Sports Word Find Puzzles*, *Dodgers Trivia*, *Cleveland Browns Trivia*, *San Francisco 49ers Trivia*, and *Detroit Tigers Trivia*, he published the monthly *Baseball Trivia Newsletter*. A nationally syndicated columnist, his weekly "Stat Sheet" is supplied to more than 600 newspapers.

JIM MURRAY, veteran sports columnist of the *Los Angeles Times*, is one of America's most acclaimed writers. He has been named "America's Best Sportswriter" by the National Association of Sportscasters and Sportswriters 14 times, was awarded the Red Smith Award, and was twice winner of the National Headliner Award. In addition, he was awarded the J. G. Taylor Spink Award in 1987 for "meritorious contributions to baseball writing." With this award came his 1988 induction into the National Baseball Hall of Fame in Cooperstown, New York.

EARL WEAVER is the winningest manager in Baltimore Orioles history by a wide margin. He compiled 1,480 victories in his 17 years at the helm. After managing eight different minor league teams, he was given the chance to lead the Orioles in 1968. Under his leadership the Orioles finished lower than second place in the American League East only four times in 17 years. One of only 12 managers in big league history to have managed in four or more World Series, Earl was named Manager of the Year in 1979. The popular Weaver had his number 5 retired in 1982, joining Brooks Robinson, Frank Robinson, and Jim Palmer, whose numbers were retired previously. Earl Weaver continues his association with the professional baseball scene by writing, broadcasting, and coaching.